"*A Jesus Easter* will help your family understand the story of Easter, from its first hint in the book of Genesis right through to the spread of the gospel in the early church. Buy a copy of this excellent book and start a tradition of taking your family through an Easter devotional every year."

MARTY MACHOWSKI, family pastor and author of *Long Story Short*

"This is such a good Easter devotional! It's richly packed with amazing truths, full of helpful questions and notes, and adaptable for a range of ages. I love the way it doesn't just show God's rescue plan but also introduces the lies of Satan in all their different forms and the promises of Jesus that combat them and help us rest in him. I'm certain it will help families focus on our Saviour and also generate further discussions about everyday faith."

TAMAR POLLARD, Director for Families, Children, and Youth Ministry, Grace Community Church, Bedford, UK

"I really enjoyed showing this to my boys! The timing was short, the process was simple, and it pointed us to the Saviour, King Jesus. I loved how it showed us God's grand design—how the Easter story is really the Jesus story and how we see the themes from the beginning of Scripture continue all the way through. Barbara reveals the lies of Satan, the truth of Jesus, and the hope of Easter."

PHIL HOWE, Scripture Union Northern Ireland

"Barbara Reaoch takes us on a fascinating journey through the Old Testament and Jesus' ministry, showing us with clarity and joy that all the Scriptures point to Jesus. A helpful guide for those wanting to understand how the Bible fits together."

THOMAS SCHREINER, Associate Dean for Scripture and Interpretation, The Southern Baptist Theological Seminary

"An engaging, Christ-exalting, gospel-centered resource for family discipleship. This devotional will introduce children to the Savior promised in Genesis and how he rescues us from sin. Celebrate Easter this year with your children by reading *A Jesus Easter* together!"

CHRISTINA FOX, author of *Tell God How You Feel*

"Celebrate the resurrection of Jesus as a family with this wonderful new 30-day devotional by best-selling author and master teacher Barbara Reaoch. Using kid-friendly language, interactive questions, and space to draw, *A Jesus Easter* explores the Bible to show how King Jesus has triumphed over the devil, sin, and death. It's the perfect addition to any Easter basket!"

CHAMP THORNTON, pastor and author of *The Radical Book for Kids*

"As a father of five, I'm grateful to have this reliable, clear, and engaging Easter devotional to help me lead my family in exploring God's amazing rescue plan in Christ alone. If you too want your family and others to treasure the truth of Jesus this Easter, pick up this book and read it together!"

BRIAN J. WRIGHT, pastor and author of *God's Daring Dozen*

"Another example of a great family devotional, which allows all ages to explore the Easter story together. With space to read, reflect, journal, and discuss together, it allows for different learning styles as well as different ages, helping you to look as a family at the greatest story of all time."

RUTH BROMLEY, Children's Development Officer, Presbyterian Church in Ireland

"*A Jesus Easter* is an interactive discipleship guide for families—one that helps adults to communicate and apply powerful gospel truths in kid-friendly language. If you're looking to cultivate meaningful conversations about Easter and its implications for everyday life, this creative resource is for you."

CHRISTINE CHAPPELL, Outreach Director and Hope + Help Podcast Host, Institute for Biblical Counseling and Discipleship

"A very effective teaching tool to help children learn about who Jesus is. It has a consistent lesson format and the journaling sections allow for individual creativity, which will leave a mental image in the mind of the child."

CAROL MCCARTY, illustrator and former educator

BARBARA REAOCH

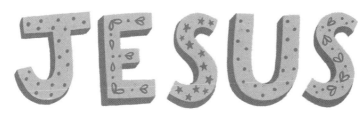

A JESUS EASTER

Explore God's Amazing Rescue Plan

thegoodbook
COMPANY

This book is lovingly dedicated to Benjamin, Stacy, Jonathan, Elizabeth, Chris, and our family's next generation.

Psalm 145:4

A Jesus Easter

Published by:
The Good Book Company

thegoodbook.com | thegoodbook.co.uk
thegoodbook.com.au | thegoodbook.co.nz | thegoodbook.co.in

Cover design and illustrations by Emma Randall | Design and art direction by André Parker

ISBN: 9781784987039 | Printed in Turkey

CONTENTS

BEFORE YOU BEGIN

These devotions are ideal for all ages. They are about faith—trusting Jesus, not your own goodness. They are about repentance—living for Jesus, not yourself. They are for children who already believe and for those who do not yet believe in Jesus. We all need encouragement all the time to believe Jesus's truth.

Prepare your own heart before you lead your family or others in *A Jesus Easter*. Ask your heavenly Father to guide you. Ask for insight about what questions to ask and how to promote discussion. Pray for God to give you a daily desire to make Jesus the focus of the run-up to Easter.

THE DAILY PATTERN

Each day has four parts: Explore, Explain, Engage, and Enter in. These are followed by a wonderful true statement about Jesus and some family journaling space.

EXPLORE

Reading the Bible passage together is the key activity. Why did Jesus come? The first 10 days explore true stories in the Old Testament which show us something about God's plan for sending Jesus. We start in the Garden of Eden, where God's family was perfect. Satan (the devil) was seen in the garden as a snake. Adam and Eve listened to the serpent's lie. Their sin broke everything. But God had a plan to make a family for himself again.

Days 11-30 explore passages in the Gospel accounts of Jesus's life, starting with his baptism and telling the whole story of Easter. We walk alongside Jesus and see how he made God's plans come true. We look forward to the day when we will be with Jesus in heaven forever as God's perfect family.

EXPLAIN

Each day three things are highlighted: God's plan for Easter, the serpent's lies, and Jesus's truth. Try to answer your child's questions but don't get bogged down in details. Assure everyone that as they learn more about Jesus, the truths will start to connect.

ENGAGE

There are two Engage questions for older children. They are designed to help children discover how each truth intersects with their lives and to stimulate deeper discussion. There are also two simpler questions ideal for younger children or those with less Bible knowledge. The older and younger questions are marked as shown below:

For older children   For younger children

Be prepared to get the conversation going. Ask God for willingness to talk about times when you are tempted to sin. Pray that you will respond to your kids with understanding and not in a judgmental tone. As your family responds honestly to God's word and Spirit, they will begin to treasure the truth of Jesus.

ENTER IN

This short prayer is a springboard for your response to whatever God shows you about himself, Jesus, and yourself.

JESUS IS...

These "Jesus is..." statements will help your family to remember each day's key truth about Jesus. Some have been decorated for you, though your child may want to add more pictures or patterns. Others have letter outlines for your child to color in.

FAMILY JOURNALING SPACE

This is a place to respond to what God has shown you. You might want to write down what you have learned, draw a picture, list things to thank God for, draw how your face looks when you think about Jesus, or use this space for any other way you want to respond to God. There is some extra journaling space at the back of the book for any days when you have an idea that needs more room.

ANSWERS

If you would find it helpful, you can download an answer sheet to all of the Explore and Engage questions from **www.thegoodbook.com/ajeaster-answers.pdf**

TIPS FOR SUCCESS

Be brief. Be real. Be consistent.

SOME USEFUL BIBLE WORDS

AMEN: This Hebrew word means "I agree." It is a way of joining in with someone's prayer.

BIBLE / SCRIPTURE / GOD'S WORD: Although the Bible was written by about 40 people, God made sure that they wrote exactly what he wanted them to write. God speaks to us through the Bible, and what he says in the Bible is always true.

DEBT: Another way of saying that you owe someone something is to say you owe them a debt. The Bible sometimes uses this word to talk about sin. We should act the way God wants. When we don't, we owe him something to make up for what we've done wrong. We can't pay this debt on our own! But when Jesus came, he paid it for us.

DISCIPLES / APOSTLES: Anyone who is Jesus's friend and follower is his disciple. The twelve men who were Jesus's closest friends are sometimes called his disciples, but they are also called his "apostles".

EASTER: God planned some important days that would change the world: the day when Jesus died (Good Friday), and the day when he came alive again (Easter Sunday). We call these days (and the lead-up to them) "Easter."

GOSPEL: The Greek word "gospel" means "good news." The gospel of Jesus is the good news that Jesus came to save us from the problem of sin.

HOSANNA: This Hebrew word is a way of saying, "You are amazing, God!"

JUDGE / JUDGMENT: A judge decides whether someone should be punished. God is the best judge because he is always right and fair. When we talk about his judgment, we either mean the decision he makes about whether someone should be punished, or the punishment itself.

KINGDOM OF GOD: This isn't a physical place. It is God's people living under his rule as their King.

MERCY: Mercy is when God doesn't treat us in the way we deserve. Instead God shows us grace, which is his huge kindness to people who don't deserve it.

PENALTY: When you do something wrong, you have to pay a penalty. It's a kind of punishment. For example, when you park in the wrong place, you might have to pay money. Or when you break the rules in a game, you might have points taken away from you. When a penalty has been paid, it means you have made up for the wrong thing you did.

PRIEST: A priest is a person who represents people to God, and God to people. In Bible times priests worked in the temple and helped people know God better.

PROPHET: A prophet is a messenger from God. They speak God's words to other people.

REPENT / REPENTANT: When you repent, you say sorry for what you have done wrong and turn away in a new direction. A repentant person is someone who has repented!

RESURRECTION: Jesus died on the first Good Friday. But he didn't stay dead! On the first Easter Sunday God raised Jesus back to life.

RIGHTEOUS / RIGHTEOUSNESS: To be righteous means to be "right with God."

SACRIFICE: When we give up something we love for the sake of someone else, we are making a sacrifice. In Bible times, people used to bring sacrifices of animals to God to show him that they loved him or that they were sorry for doing wrong. Jesus made the best-ever sacrifice: he gave up his life for our sake!

SIN / SINFUL: When we sin, we do what *we* want instead of what *God* wants. Jesus came to rescue us from the problem of sin.

SPIRIT / HOLY SPIRIT: There is only one God, but he is three persons: God the Father, God the Son (Jesus), and God the Holy Spirit. The Spirit points us to the truth about Jesus, and helps us to live the way God's word (the Bible) tells us to.

TEMPLE: In Bible times, this was a building that reminded the people that God was with them. People went there to pray and to make sacrifices.

THE CROSS: Jesus's enemies killed him by nailing him to a cross and leaving him there to die. But it was God who had already planned that Jesus would die. As Jesus died on the cross, he took all the punishment for our sin, so that everyone who trusts in Jesus can be forgiven.

WITNESS: At the most simple level, this word means somebody who sees something happen. But it also means somebody who tells other people about what they've seen or what they know. We haven't seen Jesus with our eyes, but we can still be witnesses by telling people what we know about him.

WRATH: This means God's right anger against sin.

DAY 1

GOD'S FIRST PROMISE

EXPLORE

Read Genesis 3:1-5, 14-15

Who lied to Adam and Eve? (verses 3-4)

What did God promise about the serpent? (verses 14-15)

EXPLAIN

Even before God made the world, he had a plan for Easter. God planned to make a beautiful family. He started with his first children, Adam and Eve. God built a lush garden to be their home. He talked with them like best friends talk and gave them lots of delicious fruit to eat. God loved Adam and Eve so much that he warned them not to eat the fruit of one tree. They would die if they ate that fruit.

But a serpent in the garden (who was really Satan) told them God had lied. When Adam and Eve believed Satan's lie and ate the fruit, sin broke God's perfect world. Now earthquakes and floods happen. People get sick and die. Could anything be worse? Yes! Sin infects our hearts. Now people everywhere believe the serpent's terrible lie.

Adam and Eve were so sad and afraid. But God made the best-ever promise. God would send a Rescuer so his family could know him as their own dear Father. The serpent would hurt the Rescuer. But the Rescuer would crush the serpent and free our hearts from the serpent's lie! **Jesus is the Rescuer God promised.**

ENGAGE

Obeying God brings us true happiness. But the serpent tempts us to think that God's way isn't best. When we try to find happiness without God we sin. God made us. He loves us. And God's way is always best.

- Adam and Eve were probably sad and afraid after they sinned. How do you feel after you sin?

- What is sin?

- When you feel you can't beat sin, how does God's promise of Jesus help you?

- Why is God's promise to send Jesus the best-ever promise?

ENTER IN

Heavenly Father, thank you for making us and loving us. Please help us to love you more this Easter and always. Amen.

JESUS IS THE RESCUER

FAMILY JOURNALING SPACE

IDEAS: Draw Jesus crushing the serpent; or write your own prayer; or something else…

DAY 2

SAFE FOREVER

EXPLORE

Read Genesis 6:9-13 and 9:13-16

Describe the world at the time God spoke to Noah. (6:11-13)

God flooded the whole earth with water. Afterwards, what promise did God make to Noah—and to us all? (9:15)

EXPLAIN

Was God's plan for Easter hopeless? No! Adam and Eve had turned away from God but God would never turn away from them. They did not die right away. But sin had ruined their hearts and their children's hearts and their children's children's hearts. By the time of Noah, everyone loved sin best. Not even the warning of a worldwide flood would stop people from listening to the serpent.

"Is God's judgment fair?" questions the serpent. The truth is, no one's heart hates pain and death more than God's does. God's anger against evil is right and fair. Our hearts want justice when a bully does wrong. And we can expect God to act justly when we hurt others.

The ark was God's rescue plan for Noah, his family, and all the animals. As God judged the world's evil, he kept Noah's family safe in the ark. But Noah needed a greater rescue than from the flood. Noah loved God but sin still infected his heart. Jesus is the only Rescuer from sin. On the cross, Jesus took God's right anger against evil on himself (Romans 6:23). **Jesus keeps us safe with God forever.**

ENGAGE

God's rescue plan for Noah looked forward to God's greater rescue of us through Jesus. Jesus took all our punishment. God's children can know they will never face God's judgment (Romans 8:1). God always keeps his promises.

How is the flood a rescue plan that both comforts and warns us?

Does God let evil go on forever?

What truths about God do you see in this story?

How is God the real hero of this story?

ENTER IN

Our Father, thank you for giving us a way of safety in Jesus. Help us want to be your close friend. Show our family how to help our neighbors know you and love you so that they will be safe with Jesus too. Amen.

JESUS KEEPS US SAFE

FAMILY JOURNALING SPACE

IDEAS: Draw Noah's ark; or list other things that keep people safe; or something else…

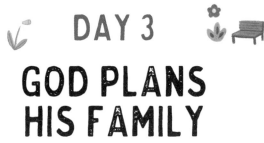

DAY 3

GOD PLANS HIS FAMILY

EXPLORE

Read Genesis 12:1-7

What did God tell Abram to do? (verse 1)

What did God promise Abram? (verses 2-3 and 7)

EXPLAIN

The long wait for Easter makes us wonder, *"What happened to God's plan for his beautiful family?"* After the flood, more and more people believed the serpent's lies. God said to Abram (later called Abraham), *"Leave your home and follow me."* Abram didn't have any children. But God promised Abram a big family! And one of Abram's children would bless the whole world. Abram trusted God.

The serpent argues, *"How can you trust a God who is so unfair? His family is just a few lucky people."* Here's the truth: God's family is bigger than we can imagine (Genesis 15:5)! If we could count the stars, we'd know the number of people in God's family. From the very beginning God planned his big, beautiful family to hold many children from every corner of the world (Revelation 7:9).

How many children are in God's family? Better to ask, "Am I God's child?" All who trust in Jesus as their Rescuer are God's children. Abram's son's son's son's … son, Jesus Christ, is God's promised blessing (Galatians 3:7-9, 14). **God makes all who trust in Jesus his child.**

ENGAGE

God's promise to Abram to bless all nations never ended. It is still real today! All who believe the truth about Jesus receive the promised blessing. They become God's child in his forever family.

- Do you think Abram was afraid to follow God? What fears keep some people from trusting God?

- Why do you think Abram was not afraid to follow God?

- What promise is God calling you to believe, by faith?

- Many people will be in God's family. Would you like to be?

ENTER IN

Father God, we want to believe your promises. We admit that we feel afraid when we don't have all the answers. Please give us faith to trust you. Amen.

JESUS MAKES US GOD'S CHILDREN

FAMILY JOURNALING SPACE

IDEAS: Draw Abram looking at the stars; or list as many nations as you can; or something else...

DAY 4

SPEAKING GOD'S WORD

EXPLORE

Read Exodus 33:7-13

Describe how Moses and the Lord spoke to one another. (verses 7-11)

What help did Moses need from the Lord? (verses 12-13)

EXPLAIN

Was Moses the Rescuer God promised to send? Moses rescued God's special family (called Israel) from their slavery in Egypt. But he could not rescue God's family from their slavery to sin. As God's prophet, Moses spoke God's true words. But Moses could not give life to their hearts. Moses told God's family to watch for The Prophet, Jesus (Deuteronomy 18:17-19; John 5:46).

After Moses, God sent other prophets to speak his word. *"Jesus is just another prophet,"* groans the serpent. The truth is, Jesus is not like any other prophet. Only Jesus is God himself. Jesus is the Word (John 1:1). Jesus's powerful word created everything, and he holds everything together (Colossians 1:15-17).

He speaks to us as we read the Bible. We hear the difference between Jesus's words (truth) and the serpent's words (lies).

Our words may be helpful. But only one person's words can rescue us from the serpent. Only one person's words can give life to our dead hearts. God said that this person is Jesus: "This is my Son … Listen to him!" (Matthew 17:5). **Jesus is our Prophet.**

ENGAGE

God was very kind to call Moses to lead his special family. Moses was a great prophet but Jesus is greater. Jesus is God's Son. Only Jesus has words that speak life into our hearts (John 11:25).

- What makes Jesus better than any other prophet?

- How is Jesus different from Moses?

- What makes the Bible different than any other book?

- How do we hear Jesus's words?

ENTER IN

Father God, thank you for sending Jesus. Help us listen to you as we read the Bible. We want to hear your words to us. Please give life and joy to our hearts. Amen.

JESUS IS OUR PROPHET

FAMILY JOURNALING SPACE

IDEAS: Draw Moses listening to God; or write how you feel about Jesus's words; or something else…

DAY 5

FRIENDS WITH GOD

EXPLORE

Read Exodus 40:12-16

Who did God choose to be priests? (verses 12-15)

How did Aaron and his sons get ready to serve God as priests? (verses 12-15)

EXPLAIN

Was Aaron the Rescuer God promised to send? The serpent's words had left God's special family—Israel—lonely, sad, and afraid. Lies, jealousy, and anger filled their hearts. They needed their Father. God's tent was close by but their Father seemed far away. Would the big, heavy curtain in God's tent keep them from him forever (Exodus 40:21)? As high priest Aaron's job was to show God's special family how to come closer to God. But Aaron could not heal their broken friendship with God.

The serpent yells, *"Who needs to be God's friend? Live for yourself and be happy."* The truth is, selfishness and sin keep us from God. God made us for himself. True happiness is loving God, living for him, and enjoying a friendship with him forever.

Aaron took the very best lamb, killed it, and put its blood on the altar behind the curtain (Leviticus 16:15-17). The sacrifice hinted at Jesus—the Lamb of God. Jesus is the only one who can truly take the place of God's guilty children. God's Lamb, Jesus, gave his own blood to mend our broken friendship with our Father (Hebrews 9:11-12). **Jesus the Lamb is our Priest.**

ENGAGE

Aaron was a great high priest but Jesus is greater. Jesus is the Priest *and* the Lamb. Jesus gave his blood for our sin so that we might enjoy our Father's love forever.

What happens when we believe the lie "live for yourself and be happy"?

What makes us truly happy?

What in this lesson helps you love God more?

Who is the Lamb of God?

ENTER IN

Father, thank you for your love. Help us see the ways you are showing us your friendship. We admit that we usually think of ourselves before you and others. Teach us how to be a friend to you and to others. Amen.

JESUS IS OUR PRIEST

FAMILY JOURNALING SPACE

IDEAS: Draw the heavy curtain and the altar in the temple; or write down what it means to you to be friends with God; or something else...

DAY 6

GOD'S CHOSEN KING

EXPLORE

Read 2 Samuel 7:4-5, 12-16

Who did God say would build a house for him? (verses 12-13)

How long will a king from David's family rule? (verses 13, 16)

EXPLAIN

Was King David the Rescuer God promised to send? David knew that God's special family (Israel) had built a beautiful tent for God. But David dreamed of building a bigger, stronger house to honor God. What a surprise when David heard God say, *"I'm going to build a house for **you**!"* Not a house of wood and stone but a family with a son who would be a king forever. From then on, God's children knew that David's son's son's son's ... son would be God's promised Rescuer, King Jesus.

*"Shouldn't God just go along with **our** plans?"* whines the serpent. It's not wrong to dream about our futures. But the truth is, even our super-sized dreams are too small compared to God's good plans for us. His word and his Spirit guide

us into his kingdom dreams. God allows us to be part of his plan which will go on forever.

King Jesus teaches us to pray, *"Father, I want your kingdom to come, and your will to be done, on earth as it is in heaven"* (Luke 11:2). We can ask for Jesus's kingdom to come into the hearts of our friends, family, and world! When God's children pray Jesus's kingdom prayers, we know he hears us. **Jesus is our King.**

ENGAGE

God gave King David a promise so much bigger than what David had imagined. God lets his children in on his forever plans that are bigger than we can imagine.

- How might knowing that God has good plans for you change what you want?

- How was God's plan better than David's?

- How will you pray for your family and friends?

- What friend will you pray for today?

ENTER IN

Father, thank you for hearing us when we pray. We don't always know what to say. A lot of times we just tell you what we want. Help us learn your kingdom prayers. We want to know you more. Amen.

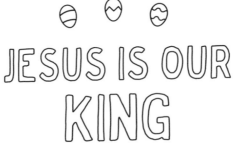

JESUS IS OUR KING

FAMILY JOURNALING SPACE

IDEAS: Draw a crown that Jesus might wear; or write your own kingdom prayer; or something else...

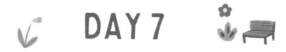

DAY 7

HARDSHIP AND HAPPINESS

EXPLORE

Read 2 Chronicles 36:15-21

How did God's special family (Israel) respond to his warnings? (verses 15-16)

Name at least four hardships God used for the good of his children. (verses 17-20)

EXPLAIN

Everything was planned for Easter. But God's family kept listening to the serpent's lies. Worse yet—they wanted to do whatever the serpent said! God loved his children too much to let them try to find happiness without him. Even though they would suffer, God had a plan to get his children back.

Enemy nations—Assyria and Babylon—marched in to capture God's family. No more king! No more land! No more temple! The serpent snaps, *"Why would God let this happen?"* The truth is, sin causes hard times. But God powerfully uses trials for his glory and for the good of his children. God's power is always superglued to his love. God's love uses every hardship to grow our happiness in him.

God's whole family suffered. Would they ever run back to him? God loved them much more than they knew. One day (a long time later), God would send his Rescuer, Jesus. Sadly, the Rescuer would be killed! Why would God let this happen? The truth is, what people planned for evil, God's powerful love planned for our good (Genesis 50:19-21). **God planned Jesus's death for our good.**

ENGAGE

The enemy nations hurt all God's family, the good and the bad. Do you wonder why God lets his children struggle even when they have not sinned? God uses our struggles for our good—to grow our faith and make us more like his Son, Jesus.

- Have you ever gone through a struggle that helped your love for God and others to grow? What happened?

- How does God show his love to us when we struggle?

- When you struggle, how does it help you to know that God's own Son suffered?

- What does this lesson help you know about God?

ENTER IN

Father God, you know us better than we understand ourselves. Help us stop fighting you. We know you love us. Please make us want to listen to your warnings and learn from you. Amen.

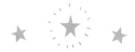

JESUS DIED FOR OUR GOOD

FAMILY JOURNALING SPACE

IDEAS: Draw a heart that shows God's love and an ear that listens to God's warnings; or write the words "power" and "love" in bubble writing, superglued together; or something else...

DAY 8

THE TREE STUMP

EXPLORE

Read Isaiah 11:1-9

Describe the new "branch" (really a person) that will come from the old stump. (verses 1-5)

What will the world be like when this "branch" rules over it? (verses 6-9)

EXPLAIN

Would the first Easter ever get here? To help his family far from home, God sent pictures of what Jesus would be like. One picture was of a tree stump. God had promised David that a son from his family would be the forever King. But enemy nations had cut down God's family. Had their sin made God break his promise? No! That tree stump was the family of Jesse, King David's father. From that stump God would bring a new king—his forever King—Jesus.

"God won't keep his promises to you. You're too bad!" accuses the serpent. The truth is, King Jesus makes bad people new from the inside out! Through the Holy

Spirit, King Jesus lives in all of God's children. The Holy Spirit gives us hearts that are happiest saying "Yes!" to whatever God says (Ezekiel 36:26-27).

One day King Jesus will return to rule God's beautiful new world. At last, life will forever be as it should—no more weeds, sickness, or death. And God's children will never believe the serpent's lies again. King Jesus will rule our hearts. We will live with God in his beautiful new world forever. **King Jesus makes us forever new.**

ENGAGE

King David's family disobeyed God. Would God take back his promise to send the Rescuer (Jesus) from David's family? No! God always keeps his promises because of who he is—not because of who we are.

Why might our sin make us doubt that God will keep his promises to us?

Who will be the King of God's beautiful new world?

How does today's lesson help you have hope?

What does Jesus make new?

ENTER IN

Father, thank you for your faithfulness. We sometimes wonder if you still want us in your family! Please help us to know you more. We want to trust you and your promises. Amen.

JESUS MAKES US NEW

FAMILY JOURNALING SPACE

IDEAS: Draw the old stump with its new branch; or describe God's beautiful new world; or something else...

DAY 9

THE SUFFERING SERVANT

EXPLORE

Read Isaiah 52:13 – 53:6

How is God's servant described? (52:13 – 53:3)

What do people think about God's servant? (53:4)

EXPLAIN

The miracle of Easter seemed far away. Had God forgotten his family? No! But the second picture of Jesus was shocking. Jesus, God's King, was also God's Suffering Servant! Jesus would enter our broken world to serve us by living and dying for us. Jesus would live the always-right life we cannot live. He would die to take the punishment we deserve (Mark 10:45).

"You don't need someone to live and die for you. Just be better!" growls the serpent. The truth is, no matter how hard we try, sin stains our hearts. Even when we do what we think is good, we do not deserve God's love.

God lovingly planned a way to punish evil and forgive his children. The priests had to kill lambs every day to give God's family forgiveness (Hebrews 10:11-14). But Jesus keeps us forever forgiven. God covers our sin-stained hearts with Jesus's always-right life (2 Corinthians 5:21). Jesus served us by living, dying, and rising from death for us. He took our punishment to give us forever forgiveness. In God's beautiful new forever world, Jesus will serve us by sharing all he has with us forever (Isaiah 53:11). **Jesus is God's Suffering Servant.**

ENGAGE

We do not deserve God's love. How can he forgive us? Jesus never sinned. He paid our penalty for sin—death. Everyone who believes this truth about Jesus receives his forgiveness. What we could never earn, Jesus freely gives: full forgiveness.

How is God's plan to forgive us different than "just be better"?

Who is God's servant?

What is the best response to God's loving plan and Jesus's amazing love?

How did Jesus's life and death serve us?

ENTER IN

Father, we confess that our hearts love other things more than you. Please forgive us. We deserve your punishment for our sin against you. Give us faith to believe that you put our sin on Jesus. Jesus, thank you for paying the death penalty in our place. Amen.

JESUS GAVE US FORGIVENESS

FAMILY JOURNALING SPACE

IDEAS: Draw Jesus switching places with you and taking your punishment; or write your favorite phrase from Isaiah 52:13 – 53:6; or something else...

DAY 10

THE HERO OF HEAVEN

EXPLORE

Read Isaiah 42:8-13

List at least five phrases about how people will rejoice when Jesus returns. (verses 10-12)

What four things will Jesus our Hero do? (verse 13)

EXPLAIN

God's family missed home. For Easter hope, God gave them a third picture of Jesus—God's Hero. Once, God had lived right in the middle of his children's neighborhood. He had welcomed them into his big, beautiful temple. Then something horrible happened! God's family tried to live without him. Enemy nations captured them. The temple was destroyed. Had God left forever?

The serpent shouts, *"Only make-believe comic-book stories have heroes."* The truth is, Jesus lived, died, and rose again—it's a fact of history. No one has ever met a comic-book superhero. Jesus is a real, live, courageous, victorious hero.

Jesus knew victory would be hard. He suffered and died to get his children back from the serpent. But he couldn't stay dead! Jesus came alive again and many people saw him (1 Corinthians 15:6). Jesus went back to his Father as the Hero of heaven. And Jesus will come back to rule God's beautiful new forever world (Isaiah 65:17-19). God's family will shout out in triumph. No more running away. No more enemies. No more serpent! Father God will bring his home to us and we will live together forever. **Jesus is our Hero.**

ENGAGE

Faith in Jesus starts with believing God's true story. Jesus really won the battle. Through his life, death, and resurrection Jesus defeated the serpent. Jesus gives us courage to live for him today.

- Next time you struggle with sharing your beliefs with friends, how can it help you to remember that Jesus is real and a hero?

- How is Jesus different than a superhero?

- With what people or in what situations do you find it hardest to live for Jesus? What do you need from Jesus to live for him?

- What is courage? Will you ask Jesus for courage to live for him?

ENTER IN

Father, thank you for giving us faith to believe that Jesus is the real hero of the universe. Until he comes again to make all things new, give us courage to live for him. Amen.

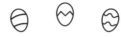

JESUS IS OUR HERO

FAMILY JOURNALING SPACE

IDEAS: Draw Jesus as a victorious hero; or write down situations where you especially need courage; or something else…

DAY 11

AN ORDINARY-LOOKING KING

EXPLORE

Read John 1:6-13

Jesus (the true light) came into the world to give God's special family (Israel) forever life. What did they think of him? (verses 9-11)

What did God give to everyone who received and believed in Jesus? (verses 12-13)

EXPLAIN

The first Easter was getting close! God had brought his special family, Israel, back home to their land. But they still wondered, *"When will God send his king?"* Then God sent John to get his family ready to meet King Jesus. John told everyone, *"Repent!"* (Luke 3:3). King Jesus would help them turn away from the wrong things they thought, said, and did. But God's family didn't want Jesus. He didn't wear royal robes or a jeweled crown.

"How could someone so ordinary be God's King?" questions the serpent. The truth is, Jesus is God himself! Jesus spoke light and life into the world (John 1:3-5). And he shines light and life into our hearts (2 Corinthians 4:6).

Before the beginning of everything, God set his heart on a beautiful new family. But God's family is different than people think. Anyone who believes Jesus is their Rescuer and King belongs to God's family. God opens the eyes of our hearts to believe Jesus is his Son (Ephesians 1:18). We become his children and enjoy the loving oneness the Father, Son, and Holy Spirit have always enjoyed. **Jesus makes our hearts alive.**

ENGAGE

Faith is more than believing facts about Jesus. Our minds know that Jesus is the Son of God. He died on the cross to pay for our sin, was buried, and rose again. And with our hearts we believe God's promises. We know that receiving Jesus means we are God's child forever.

What does it mean to be God's child?

Who shines light into our hearts?

Why do you think we need God's help to believe Jesus is our Rescuer and King?

How do we become God's child?

ENTER IN

Father God, we know you can shine through the darkness in our hearts. Please give us faith to believe the truth about Jesus. We want to be your children forever. Amen.

JESUS GIVES US LIGHT AND LIFE

FAMILY JOURNALING SPACE

IDEAS: Draw a candle shining light into a dark place; or write what it means to you to be God's child; or something else…

DAY 12
MARY'S GIFT

EXPLORE

Read John 12:1-8

How do Judas's words about Mary's gift show us what he loves? (verses 4-6)

How does Mary's gift show us what *she* loves? (verses 3 and 7-8)

EXPLAIN

Jesus helped his friends get ready for Easter. Lazarus had died. His sisters Mary and Martha were so sad. Then Jesus gave Lazarus life again! How could Lazarus, Mary, and Martha share their happiness and love for Jesus? They threw a party! All his friends, even Judas, came for dinner. But what was that sweet smell filling the house? Mary had poured out her very expensive perfume on Jesus's feet. Why?

"True happiness comes through what you have and what you do," howls the serpent. The truth is, life with God is the only way to true happiness. Having money, friends, or talents may make us happy for a while. But we always want to have or do or be *more*. Jesus came to fill our hearts with his life. He fills us with true satisfaction (John 10:10).

When Jesus raised Lazarus he said, "I am the resurrection and the life" (John 11:25). Now, Mary quietly poured out her most costly gift. Her heart shouted, *"Jesus, I believe you are my Rescuer and King. I love you with my life!"* Judas had believed the serpent's lie. He was wrong. Mary was truly happy. **Jesus gives true happiness.**

ENGAGE

Jesus was Mary's true happiness. He came to give his life for her. Now she could give her life to him—her hands, feet, eyes, tongue, mind, and heart. Nothing Judas had or did could ever have given him true happiness. Only Jesus makes us happy forever.

- God wants to change what we think and do, but most of all, he wants to change what we love. Why, do you think?

- Why did Mary pour perfume on Jesus's feet?

- What does it look like to live your life for Jesus?

- Who gives us true happiness—forever?

ENTER IN

Father God, help us see if we are looking for happiness in ways that do not please you. Please give us more love for Jesus. We want to love him with all that we are and all that we have. Amen.

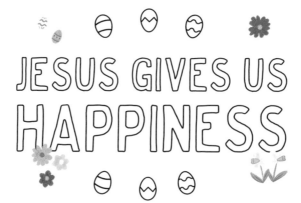

JESUS GIVES US HAPPINESS

FAMILY JOURNALING SPACE

IDEAS: Draw a jar like Mary's and fill it with things that show you love Jesus; or write a prayer to tell Jesus you love him; or something else…

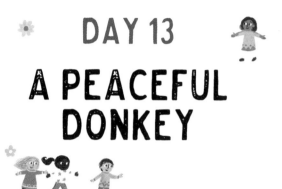

DAY 13

A PEACEFUL DONKEY

EXPLORE

Read John 12:12-18

Many people went out to see Jesus on his way to Jerusalem. What did they shout? (verse 13)

What was written long before about Jesus riding a donkey? (verse 15)

EXPLAIN

Finally—only one week until the first Easter! Like every year, God's family came to Jerusalem for Passover. Everyone heard that Jesus had raised Lazarus to life. Would Jesus use his amazing power to fight the Romans? The Roman soldiers made life so hard for God's family. Some of God's family shouted, *"Jesus is the king we want!"* When he rode into Jerusalem on a donkey, they cheered. They waved palm branches and yelled, "Hosanna!" (Psalm 118:25-26)

Why would God send his King on a donkey? Wouldn't God's King come on a battle-ready horse instead of a peaceful donkey? The shrewd serpent asks,

"What makes you think God will give you what you want?" The truth is, God does *not* always give us what we want.

God's family wanted a king to defeat their enemy. They didn't see that their sin was a bigger enemy. God gives us something better than what we want. God sent Jesus to take our punishment on himself. Jesus defended us from God's right anger against sin. God covered us with Jesus's always-rightness. Now, because of Jesus, we can run to God! **Jesus gives us what is best: peace with God.**

ENGAGE

The Bible says that our sin makes us God's enemies (Romans 5:10). Jesus knew that only his death and resurrection would give us peace with God. Just think—because of Jesus we can have a forever friendship with the Father!

- Why do you think peace with God is what we need more than anything? How does Jesus make a way for us to enjoy this peace?

- How did the people want Jesus to help them?

- Who do you know who you would like to have peace with God?

- What did Jesus give the people (and us) that was better than they wanted?

ENTER IN

Father God, when we don't get what we want, it's hard! We need your help to see the good you want to give us. Please grow our love for the true peace that Jesus gives. Amen.

JESUS GIVES US PEACE

FAMILY JOURNALING SPACE

IDEAS: Draw a peaceful donkey; or write about why God's peace is the best thing we could have; or something else...

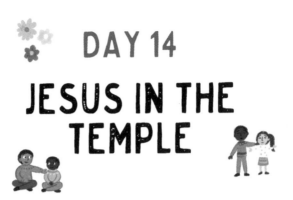

DAY 14

JESUS IN THE TEMPLE

EXPLORE

Read Matthew 21:12-17

Why did Jesus make all the money-changers leave the temple? (verse 13)

How did the religious leaders react when they saw the wonderful things Jesus did? (verse 15)

EXPLAIN

Easter was one day closer. Crowds filled Jerusalem. At Passover all God's family visited his home—the temple. Everyone came with the blood of a lamb. They wanted to meet with God. But there was a big problem! The temple was like a busy shopping mall. Even worse, money-changers cheated people. These cheaters hadn't come to meet with God—so Jesus made them leave!

Everyone watched as the coins rolled out of sight, animals got loose, and birds flew away. The serpent roars, *"Who does Jesus think he is?"* But Jesus had told everyone the truth about himself: "Destroy this temple, and I will raise it again in three days" (John 2:19).

What did Jesus mean? Jesus spoke of his own body (John 2:21). After he died and rose to life, people would know that Jesus is God's Son. Jesus is God's true temple. We meet with God through Jesus! He makes our hearts his home (1 Corinthians 6:19). He is never far away. Jesus invites us to talk with him like best friends talk. He even hears our thoughts. He sees everything about us and still loves us. **Jesus, God's Son, makes our hearts his home.**

ENGAGE

What could be better than going to the temple to meet with God? The temple coming to us! Now Jesus lives in everyone who believes in him. We are God's temple (2 Corinthians 6:16). In Jesus, the temple is with us always.

- What helps you the most about knowing that Jesus makes your heart his home?

- What was God's temple supposed to be for?

- What things help us enjoy our closeness with Jesus? Tell about a time when you felt close to him.

- Who is God's temple today?

ENTER IN

Father God, we're amazed that you love us and want to talk with us. Please forgive us for letting other things get in the way of time with you. Help us set a time to spend with you each day! Amen.

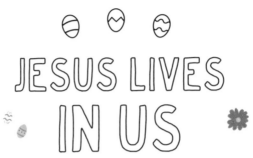

JESUS LIVES IN US

FAMILY JOURNALING SPACE

IDEAS: Draw yourself and Jesus talking together; or write a prayer inviting Jesus to live in your heart; or something else...

DAY 15
BETRAYAL!

EXPLORE

Read Luke 22:1-6

Who was looking for a way to get rid of Jesus? (verse 2)

What did they agree to give Judas if he would help them? (verse 5)

EXPLAIN

The first Easter was almost here! Time for God's promise to come to light: though the serpent would hurt the Rescuer, the Rescuer would crush the serpent and free our hearts from the serpent's lie (Genesis 3:15). People crowded the streets to hear Jesus teach about God. But the religious leaders were jealous. The people loved Jesus—not them! If only the people would trust them, not God. The leaders decided to kill Jesus. Judas would help them.

The sly serpent squawks, *"How can you trust God if he lets bad things happen?"* The truth is, we can trust God's good purposes. Even when we don't understand, he gives us all we need and more. God never deserves blame for people's evil actions. He always deserves our praise.

Judas was not a puppet. He chose to love money more than God (John 12:4-6). Judas believed his feelings more than God's word and fell into the serpent's trap.

Soon, Judas would betray Jesus to the religious leaders for 30 pieces of silver (Matthew 26:14-16). Judas acted in an evil way. He was guilty. But God worked out his plan through Judas. At the cross, Jesus crushed the serpent's lie. **Jesus proves we can trust God always.**

ENGAGE

The serpent tempts us to love money, trust in our own efforts, and believe his lies. When we choose to trust anything more than God and the Bible, just like Judas, we are to blame. But we have a choice! Because of Jesus we can choose to cry out to God for forgiveness.

- What lies did Judas believe that impacted the choices he made?

- What were some of Judas's wrong choices?

- How does knowing the truth about God and Jesus impact the choices you make?

- How did God use Judas as part of his plan?

ENTER IN

Father God, you are right in all you do. Help us remember to ask you for help when the serpent tempts us. Help us trust you with the hard things in our lives. We want to love you more. Amen.

JESUS PROVES WE CAN TRUST GOD

FAMILY JOURNALING SPACE

IDEAS: Draw Judas counting his money; or list some times when God helped you make a good choice; or something else…

DAY 16

THE LAST SUPPER

EXPLORE

Read Luke 22:14-20

Who did Jesus eat his last Passover meal with? (verse 14)

How are the cup and the bread a picture of Jesus? (verses 19-20)

EXPLAIN

Easter would change everything! Every year God's family ate lamb at a special meal called Passover. God wanted the meal to remind them of how he had saved them from slavery in Egypt (Exodus 12). Now, something new and greater was about to happen. Jesus, the Lamb of God, would save us from slavery to sin (John 1:29). Today, we eat the Lord's Supper (Communion). We remember that Jesus's blood saves us from the forever sadness of loving our own way. His broken body fills us with his life, to live a truly happy life with him.

"How can Jesus really fill us with his life? No one can really know him," moans the serpent. The truth is, God made us to hear Jesus's voice deep within us,

in our hearts. We do not hear a sound—we hear God speaking to us when we read the Bible. And we see Jesus's life working through us to live for him.

To know Jesus is to enjoy him and life too! Jesus is coming back! In his new, beautiful, forever world, Jesus will eat this supper again—with us (Revelation 19:6-8)! God's children will be a happier happy than ever before (Revelation 7:16-17). What a great day! **Jesus invites us to know him and live with him now and forever.**

ENGAGE

God made us to know him as our Father and love him forever. Through the Holy Spirit, Jesus is alive in us. He gives us strength to live for God. Only life with God, as his children, can satisfy us forever.

- How does being God's child impact the way you live?

- What does Jesus want us to remember about him?

- How do you see Jesus's life in you—helping you to change and live a truly happy life?

- What does it mean to know Jesus and live for him?

ENTER IN

Father God, we praise you for Jesus. Jesus, you are the Lamb of God, who takes away our sin. Help us remember to ask you for help to live for you. Help us to love you more. Amen.

JESUS GIVES US LIFE WITH HIM

FAMILY JOURNALING SPACE

IDEAS: Draw the cup and the bread; or write about what it will be like to live with Jesus forever; or something else...

DAY 17

FAITH THAT NEVER FAILS

EXPLORE

Read Matthew 26:31-35

What did Peter say when Jesus warned that all the disciples would run away? (verse 33)

What did Peter say when Jesus said he would disown him three times? (verse 35)

EXPLAIN

Before the first Easter, Jesus warned his friends of danger. The serpent, with all his lies, would try to steal their faith in Jesus. The serpent had already destroyed Judas. Peter was next on his list. Peter believed that Jesus was God's Son and his Rescuer. Jesus promised to pray that Peter's faith in him "may not fail" (Luke 22:31-34). But Peter boasted, *"I will never fall away!"* Did Peter think his faith was strong enough to hold on to Jesus?

When we think our faith is strong, the serpent whispers, *"You'll never sin in that way. You're too good!"* The truth is, the strength of our faith doesn't rescue us—

Jesus rescues us. No matter how strong our faith is, we always need Jesus. Jesus our strong Rescuer, holds on to us!

Later, how sad Peter was that he had listened to the serpent (Matthew 26:69-75). Peter learned he always needed Jesus's help (1 Peter 5:8-11). Did he need to ask Jesus to save him again? No! When Peter turned back to Jesus, Jesus welcomed him with love. Peter followed Jesus with joy and his faith grew (John 21:15-23). **Jesus holds on to us forever.**

ENGAGE

Like Peter, all God's children wrestle with sinful habits. But Jesus has broken the serpent's power to control us. Sin sometimes makes us feel safe or happy for a while. But Jesus gives us a greater joy that lasts forever—loving him.

- How can you help a friend who doubts if they are God's child?

- Who rescues us from sin?

- Peter learned that he needed Jesus's help. What help do you need to ask Jesus for?

- Do we hold on to Jesus or does he hold on to us?

ENTER IN

Father God, we need you! Help save us from the serpent's power to control our thoughts, words, and actions. Please fill our minds and hearts with the truth of who you are and the truth of your word. Amen.

JESUS HOLDS US

FAMILY JOURNALING SPACE

IDEAS: Draw Jesus's hands holding on to you; or write about how Peter felt when Jesus welcomed him back; or something else...

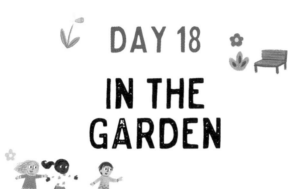

DAY 18

IN THE GARDEN

EXPLORE

Read Luke 22:39-46

What did Jesus tell his disciples to do? (verse 40)

When Jesus faced temptation, what did he ask his Father? (verse 42)

EXPLAIN

Long before the first Easter, Jesus knew he would die for us. Thorns and nails would hurt him terribly. Could anything be more painful? Yes! Worse than nails, Jesus would take God's right anger for all our sins on himself. Jesus had always been closer than close to his Father. On the cross our sin would separate Jesus from his Father. On the night before Jesus died, his heart broke. He cried to his Father, *"Is there some other way to rescue your children?"*

The serpent quarrels, *"If Jesus never sinned, how can he help you when you are tempted?"* The truth is, as a child and as a man, Jesus learned to trust and obey his Father (Hebrews 5:8). Adam and Eve sinned when the serpent tempted them. But Jesus said "No" to all the serpent's lies. How did Jesus stay strong? God gave him—and all his children—three gifts: his word, his Spirit, and prayer.

Jesus said, *"Not what I want but what you want, Father."* Sinless Jesus paid for our sins (Hebrews 2:17). He understands our struggle (Hebrews 4:15-16). He gives us all we need in every temptation all our days (Hebrews 2:18). **Jesus helps when we are tempted.**

ENGAGE

Jesus understands our temptation. God's children ask for Jesus's help. He gives us strength to obey our Father.

- Next time you are tempted to be angry, lie, cheat, be greedy, or (fill in the blank), how can knowing that Jesus gives us all we need in every temptation help you?

- Who was tempted in every way we are, but never sinned?

- When your friends are tempted, how could you use what you know about Jesus to encourage them?

- How does Jesus help us to obey our Father God?

ENTER IN

Father God, you have given us everything we need to obey you. Thank you Jesus for always saying "No" to sin. We admit that we often fall for the serpent's lies and our own desires. Sound an alarm in our hearts to ask you for help when we are tempted. Amen.

JESUS HELPS US IN TEMPTATION

FAMILY JOURNALING SPACE

IDEAS: Draw Jesus in the garden; or write your own prayer asking Jesus for help in temptation; or something else...

DAY 19

THE PLAN UNFOLDS

EXPLORE

Read Matthew 26:47-56

What signal did Judas give to the armed crowd who came to arrest Jesus? (verses 48-49)

How was Jesus's plan different than his friend's plan? (verses 51-54)

EXPLAIN

The first Easter was so close. What about God's plan to crush the serpent? Was the serpent winning? Judas led the soldiers to Jesus. They brought clubs and swords—ready for a fight. Peter was ready to fight, too (John 18:10). He even cut off a soldier's ear! Right away, Jesus healed the soldier. Then he told Peter, *"God's plan will not happen this way."*

"How can anyone understand God's plan? The Bible is just a lot of different stories," cries the serpent. The truth is, God gives us the Bible to tell us his plan. In the Bible, we see how God crushes the serpent and rescues his children.

Now, when we ask him, God opens our minds and hearts. He lets us see his plan for his Son and his beautiful new forever family.

That night, the soldiers and Jesus's friends had different plans than Jesus. Did they think they were wiser than Jesus? An army of angels watched, ready to help Jesus. The angels were so excited to see God's plan unfold (1 Peter 1:12). Jesus knew God's plan was best. **Jesus followed God's plan for us.**

ENGAGE

God's word tells us that he always planned to send Jesus to rescue us. He always planned for Jesus to die and rise to new life for us. Jesus did everything just as God planned, to make us God's children. Just as God planned, everyone who trusts in Jesus belongs to his beautiful new forever family.

- Re-enact the story of Jesus's arrest. Include Jesus's words from verses 53-54.

- Re-enact the part of the story when Jesus tells Peter to put away his sword.

- How does understanding that the Bible tells one story and not lots of different stories help you?

- Name at least one promise in the Bible that Jesus came to fulfill. (Look back through this book to help you.)

ENTER IN

Father God, all through the Bible you show us your awesome plan to send a Rescuer. Jesus, thank you for living out God's plan all the way to the cross. You alone can free our hearts from the serpent's lie. Help us love you more. Amen.

JESUS FOLLOWED GOD'S PLAN

FAMILY JOURNALING SPACE

IDEAS: Draw the soldiers who came to arrest Jesus; or list some promises which Jesus fulfilled; or something else...

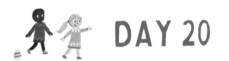

DAY 20

THE COURTROOM

EXPLORE

Read Luke 22:66-71

Who thought they were good enough to judge Jesus? (verse 66)

What did Jesus tell the religious leaders about himself? (verses 67-70)

EXPLAIN

Before the first Easter something very sad happened. The religious leaders believed the serpent's lies! They thought they were best—good enough to judge Jesus! But Jesus is the Judge. Jesus showed them the truth about their hearts (John 8:42-45). But they thought, *"We don't need forgiveness."* They did not believe that Jesus was the Rescuer God promised. *"Let's kill him,"* they decided.

The serpent scolds, *"You don't need forgiveness—just be good."* The truth is, we could never deserve God's forgiveness by what we do. God loves us, not because we deserve it, but because of Jesus (1 John 4:10). God's forgiveness is a gift. What good news! Jesus paid for God's gift to us with his life when he died on the cross (Ephesians 2:8).

When Jesus rose again, he sat down with his Father in heaven, just like he said. We can believe what Jesus tells us about himself and about our sin. Jesus is the true Judge: he is always right. Our goodness can't add to Jesus's good work for us. Our Father freely forgives his children (2 Peter 3:9). **Jesus gives us joy-filled forgiveness.**

ENGAGE

God is dishonored when people refuse to ask him for forgiveness. He wants us to say sorry for the wrong things we think and say and do. And he wants us to run to him when we sin. Jesus longs to forgive us and help us to change.

- Sometimes we have a hard time thinking of sins to confess and asking for forgiveness. Why do you think this is?

- Who is the real judge—the religious leaders or Jesus?

- Take a moment to think quietly: are you trying to carry the sadness of any sin alone? Will you confess this to Jesus and receive his joy-filled forgiveness?

- What does Jesus give to all who confess their sin?

ENTER IN

Father God, thank you for sending Jesus to take our full punishment for our sins. Please help us admit and confess our sin to you. The burden of guilt and shame is so heavy. The freedom of your forgiveness is filled with joy! Amen.

JESUS GIVES US FORGIVENESS

FAMILY JOURNALING SPACE

IDEAS: Draw the chief priests and the teachers of the law; or write words that say how you feel when you've been forgiven; or something else…

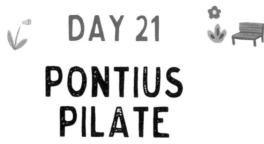

DAY 21

PONTIUS PILATE

EXPLORE

Read John 18:33-38

Who wanted Jesus to be judged by Pilate? (verse 35)

Why did Jesus come into the world? (verse 37)

EXPLAIN

God's plan for Easter included a Roman ruler named Pilate. The religious leaders did not want to believe the truth that Jesus was God's true King! They said Jesus was a criminal who lied and deserved to die. But the right to carry out the death penalty belonged to the Roman government. If Pilate knew Jesus claimed to be a king, would he kill Jesus (Luke 23:2)? Or would Pilate listen to the truth?

"What is truth?" screams the serpent through Pilate's words. The truth is, everyone can know the truth. Jesus is the truth! Many other teachers get some things right, but only Jesus gets everything right. Only Jesus is fully God and fully man. We can only know God through Jesus. We can only become God's child through faith in Jesus (John 14:6). Only Jesus makes our hearts and all things forever new.

Pilate stood before Jesus, the King over all the kings of the earth (Revelation 1:5). What if Pilate had believed God's truth—Jesus? King Jesus would have rescued him. Pilate would have become the Father's child in his beautiful family. Pilate would have entered God's forever kingdom. **Jesus is God's truth.**

ENGAGE

The powerful ruler Pilate thought he was Jesus's judge. How wrong! Pilate lived by the serpent's lies. How could he judge Jesus, the truth? Only Jesus, fully God and fully man, could say, "I am … the truth" (John 14:6).

- What are some lies you hear about God today? What truth about Jesus needs to replace these lies?

- Who was Pilate?

- How might you encourage friends, family, and neighbors with the truth about Jesus?

- What if Pilate had believed God's truth—Jesus?

ENTER IN

Father God, many people today are like Pilate when they ask, "What is truth?" Help me to believe the truth and live the truth that Jesus is your truth. Give me courage to speak for you today. Amen.

JESUS IS THE TRUTH

FAMILY JOURNALING SPACE

IDEAS: Draw Pilate asking questions; or write the word "Truth" in bubble writing; or something else...

DAY 22

THE CRIMINAL WHO WENT FREE

EXPLORE

Read Luke 23:13-20 and 23-25

Why did Pilate want to release Jesus? (verses 13-16)

How did the crowd respond to Pilate? What happened as a result? (verses 23-25)

EXPLAIN

Barabbas was part of God's Easter plan. Barabbas had robbed and killed people. Every year during Passover, Pilate let the people choose one prisoner to free (Mark 15:6). Pilate thought the people would want to free Jesus. Jesus had never done anything wrong. But Barabbas was set free, not Jesus. Jesus was determined to rescue us. He knew dying on the cross was the only way for us to be God's children—free from sin.

The serpent scoffs, *"Once Jesus sets you free, it doesn't matter how you live."* The truth is, Jesus sets us free from sin so we can live for him. Now we are free to live like Jesus. We think, speak, and love like Jesus (Romans 8:29). What can force God's children to sin? Not the lying serpent! Not anybody or anything!

God gives us a new heart to love him. We are truly free—free not to sin. His word and his Spirit teach us to love his ways. God even uses temptations to make us grow stronger (James 4:7-8). God's pleasure with us gives our hearts joy. **Jesus sets us free to live for him.**

ENGAGE

Every day we are all tempted to do wrong. But God's children no longer have to say yes to sin. Our loving Father shows us the way to go free when we are tempted (1 Corinthians 10:13). Now we can say NO to the serpent and to sin.

- When are you most tempted to sin? Why?

- Who gives us the real freedom we need?

- When you know that Jesus sets us free to live for him, how does it change the way you think about temptation?

- What is the real freedom we need?

ENTER IN

Father God, thank you for the joy of living for you. Although we are your children, we so easily give in to temptation. Teach us how to resist sin. Amen.

JESUS SETS US FREE

FAMILY JOURNALING SPACE

IDEAS: Draw chains being broken; or write how it makes you feel to be set free by Jesus; or something else...

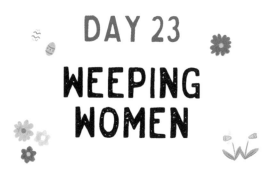

DAY 23

WEEPING WOMEN

EXPLORE

Read Luke 23:26-31

How did the women following Jesus react when they saw his cuts and bruises? (verse 27)

Who did Jesus tell them to cry for instead of him? Why? (verses 28-30)

EXPLAIN

God planned for the Passover crowds to see the first Easter. The soldiers whipped Jesus. Women saw his cuts and bruises. They cried. Jesus told them to cry for themselves, not him. They did not need to feel sorry for him—they needed to repent, quickly. Soon it would be too late: God would pour out his strong and right anger against Jerusalem for how the people had treated Jesus. A bigger judgment is coming when God will pour out his strong and right anger against *all* sin. But Jesus will rescue everyone who believes he is God's King.

"If God really loves everyone, why doesn't he just forgive them?" taunts the serpent. The truth is, sin ruins the beautiful friendship God made us for, like a

drop of poison ruins a glass of water. But God's love is so great. On the cross God made Jesus to be our hiding place. God poured out on Jesus his strong and right anger against sin. Now God gives his children mercy and keeps them from hell.

One day Jesus will return as God's Judge (Revelation 6:12-17). There will be no place to hide. No excuses. No way to cover our sins. All God's children run to him for safety now. **Jesus is our only hiding place.**

ENGAGE

No one will ever stand before God and say they never sinned. But if you trust Jesus as your Rescuer, you do not need to fear God's right anger against sin. Jesus will be your hiding place from the coming wrath.

How does this lesson help you know and love God more?

What ruins our beautiful friendship with God?

Why are the truths about Jesus in this lesson both comforting and challenging?

Who will Jesus rescue?

ENTER IN

Father God, you are right and just. Your warnings come from your heart of love. Please help us replace the lies we've believed about sin with your truth. Thank you for sending Jesus to be our hiding place. Amen.

JESUS IS OUR HIDING PLACE

FAMILY JOURNALING SPACE

IDEAS: Draw a safe hiding place; or write down some sins you feel sad about and ask Jesus to forgive you; or something else...

DAY 24

THREE CROSSES

EXPLORE

Read Luke 23:32-33 and 39-43

Why were the two men with Jesus going to be executed? (verse 32)

What truth about Jesus did one criminal know? (verses 40-41)

EXPLAIN

Two criminals nailed to crosses near Jesus were part of God's plan for Easter. One of them angrily yelled at Jesus, *"If you are really the Rescuer, save us!"* But the other criminal knew he deserved his punishment. He saw how good Jesus was. He knew Jesus had done nothing wrong. He believed Jesus was God's King. He wanted to be with Jesus in heaven. Was it too late for God to forgive him?

"You can't go to heaven. Your sins are too big for God to forgive," accuses the serpent. The truth is, Jesus forgives everyone who repents and wants to love him more than their sin (Acts 3:19). God promises to forgive his children no matter what their sin. Our heavenly Father keeps us in his beautiful family forever.

The repentant criminal knew that Jesus decides who goes to heaven. He asked Jesus, *"Will you take me with you to heaven?"* Jesus said, *"Yes, today you will be with me in heaven."* Jesus was dying on the cross to make this criminal—and everyone who trusts him—God's child forever. **Jesus opens our way to heaven.**

ENGAGE

Only God truly knows our hearts. He sees the sins we hide from others and even the sins we hide from ourselves. In kindness he helps us to repent. To repent means to have a heart that listens to God and asks his forgiveness and his help to change. It is always right to repent.

What would you tell a friend who thinks their sin is too big for God to forgive?

What difference do you see between the two criminals?

How does it make you feel to know that Jesus promises heaven to all who ask for his forgiveness?

Are any sins too big for God to forgive?

ENTER IN

Father God, most of the time we just try to cover up our sin with excuses. Please help us want to listen to you and ask for your forgiveness when you show us our sin. Amen.

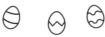

JESUS OPENS THE WAY TO HEAVEN

FAMILY JOURNALING SPACE

IDEAS: Draw the second criminal going to heaven with Jesus; or list as many things that God forgives as you can think of; or something else…

DAY 25

THE CURTAIN TEARS

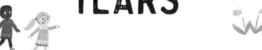

EXPLORE

Read Luke 23:44-49

Describe what happened at the time Jesus died. (verses 44-46)

What did the centurion do and say when he saw Jesus on the cross? (verse 47)

EXPLAIN

Jesus had always been closer than close to his Father. So Jesus knew God's time for Easter had come. Now the full storm of God's right anger against sin rained down on Jesus. The sun hid, warning of God's judgment. Long, long before—even before God made the sun—the Father, Son, and Holy Spirit had lovingly planned Easter. The cross was the only way for God to make his beautiful family (Galatians 4:4-5). The serpent struck Jesus. But Jesus crushed the serpent to free our hearts from the serpent's lie.

The serpent sneers, *"Can you be sure Jesus's death really pays for all your sins?"* The truth is, yes! God fully forgives everyone who repents and trusts in Jesus. On the cross, Jesus paid for all your sin—past, present, and future. Jesus said,

"It is finished!" (John 19:30). Jesus paid. God will never make you pay again (Hebrews 9:24-26).

The Father tore the big, heavy temple curtain that kept people away from him. He opened the way for us to become his children. Jesus's blood mended our broken friendship with God. Now we are free to enjoy the loving oneness the Father, Son, and Holy Spirit have always enjoyed. **Jesus fully paid for all our sin.**

ENGAGE

"It is finished!" (John 19:30). Jesus did everything he promised. So the Father tore the temple curtain open for us. The huge debt of our sin had kept us from God. We could not pay this debt. But Jesus paid our huge debt with his blood.

- If a friend paid for your ticket to a concert, you would thank them. But if you owed someone ten million dollars and a friend paid it all for you, you'd never stop thanking them! How does it make you feel to know that Jesus fully paid the debt you could never pay so you could have the greatest gift ever?

- What does the torn curtain show us?

- Look back at Day 5. Why is Jesus a better priest than Aaron?

- What did Jesus say when he finished paying for all your sin?

ENTER IN

Father God, thank you for loving us so much that you planned Easter. Jesus, thank you for paying the huge debt we could never pay to give us the greatest gift we could ever dream of. Help us know and love you more. Amen.

JESUS PAID FOR SIN FULLY

FAMILY JOURNALING SPACE

IDEAS: Draw the curtain tearing in two; or list words that describe how you feel about Jesus paying for your sin; or something else...

DAY 26

THE TOMB

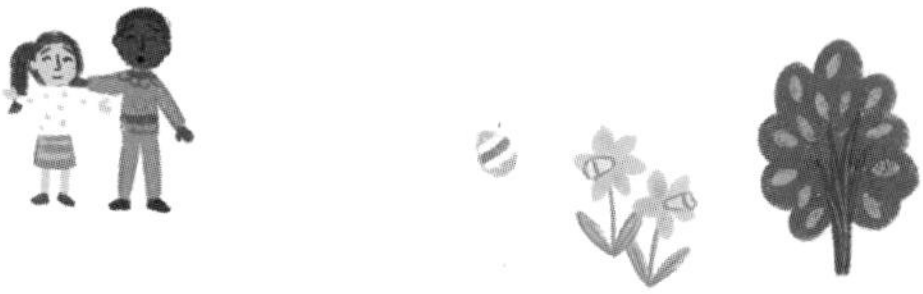

EXPLORE

Read Matthew 27:57-61

List everything we learn about Joseph in verses 57-60.

Who watched Joseph from opposite the tomb? (verse 61)

EXPLAIN

A religious leader named Joseph was part of God's plan for Easter. He knew Jesus was the King God had promised. Jesus had promised forever life. But Jesus was dead. Did Joseph wonder why Jesus had died? Joseph wrapped Jesus's dead body in a special cloth and placed it in his own new tomb (Isaiah 53:9).

The serpent jeers, *"If Jesus died, how can he promise us forever life?"* The truth is, Jesus won the battle over death. He died to rescue us from death and to destroy death (1 Corinthians 15:20-26). No more fear of punishment! The serpent can't call God's children sinners anymore (Hebrews 2:14-17).

God made us to live with him forever. But Adam and Eve believed the serpent's lie and sin broke God's perfect world. Flowers, bugs, pets, and people—all living things—die. But death cannot hold God's children. Jesus broke death's power.

God's children enjoy a forever life with God today, in heaven, and in his forever kingdom. Jesus promises that when death closes our eyes, our eyes will open to see him in heaven (John 14:2-3). **Jesus rescues us from death's power.**

ENGAGE

Death is not good! But God's children need not fear. Not even a sparrow falls to the ground outside of our Father's tender care. We each will live for all the time God has planned for us. And life in heaven is even better than the best that earth can offer (Philippians 1:21).

- After a friend who trusted Jesus dies, why do we still feel sad even though we know they are with Jesus?

- Who wrapped Jesus's dead body and placed it in his own new tomb?

- What an awesome place awaits God's children! How can knowing the truth about heaven help you today?

- What is the reason we do not need to fear death?

ENTER IN

Father God, you sent Jesus to die and win the battle over death for us. Please replace our fear of death with faith in you. Help us think about the beauty of heaven more. Show us who to comfort with these truths about you this week. Amen.

JESUS RESCUES US FROM DEATH

FAMILY JOURNALING SPACE

IDEAS: Draw Jesus's tomb; or write a prayer for someone who has lost a person they love; or something else...

DAY 27

BACK TO LIFE FOREVER

EXPLORE

Read Matthew 28:1-10

How was the women's reaction to the angel of the Lord different from the guards' reaction? (verses 4, 8)

As the women hurried away, who met them and what did he say? (verses 9-10)

EXPLAIN

No one knew Easter had come. Three days earlier, Jesus had died on the cross. Then before the sun rose, two friends, both named Mary, walked to Jesus's tomb. Their hearts thought, *"We'll never talk to Jesus again."* Then the earth shook. An angel rolled the heavy stone from the tomb. The women heard the happiest news ever: *"Jesus isn't dead anymore—he is alive!"*

"Why should we believe that Jesus came back to life?" hisses the serpent. The truth is, many people saw Jesus after his resurrection. For 40 days, they talked with him and even ate with him (Luke 24:42-43). Over 500 people together saw the resurrected Jesus (1 Corinthians 15:3-8). How could Jesus come back to life? Death could not keep Jesus in the grave because Jesus never sinned.

Suddenly the women heard Jesus's voice! Easter had come! Jesus was really alive. Now they knew—all Jesus's words were true. Jesus mends our friendship with God. We won't ever be alone. We can talk with Jesus like best friends talk. He will never leave us (John 14:16-18). **Jesus died and came back to life—forever!**

ENGAGE

Faith in Jesus is not wishful thinking. Jesus really is the Son of God! He died on the cross to pay for our sin. He was buried and rose again on the third day to give us life forever with him. He really is alive! Faith in Jesus is trusting the truth.

- How can you be sure that Jesus is alive today?

- Is Jesus alive today?

- When the women heard Jesus they knew he was alive! How does knowing that you are talking to a real live person help you to pray? What will you ask Jesus for today?

- What is it like for God's children to talk to Jesus?

ENTER IN

Father God, we know you are real. But sometimes we feel our prayers are like speaking into air. Help us remember that you are a person. You hear our every word and even the words in our mind. We want to have a real friendship with you. Amen.

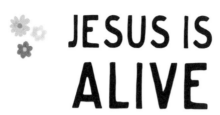

JESUS IS ALIVE

FAMILY JOURNALING SPACE

IDEAS: Draw Jesus coming back to life; or use bubble writing to write some words that describe how the women felt; or something else...

DAY 28

THE PLAN REVEALED

EXPLORE

Read Luke 24:13-21, 25-27, and 30-32 (or enjoy the whole story: Luke 24:13-35)

What did Jesus tell the two disciples about the Messiah? (verses 25-27)

When did the disciples know it was Jesus speaking to them? (verses 30-32)

EXPLAIN

It was the first Easter—but not everyone knew. Two of Jesus's friends were so sad. Jesus came to walk with them. But they didn't even recognize him! Then Jesus explained how God's word tells one story—the story of God making his beautiful new family. God always planned for Jesus to die and rise to new life to rescue us. Jesus spoke words of life, and happiness filled their hearts.

The serpent scorns, *"What a boring story."* The truth is, living with God forever will be more exciting than anything in this life (Revelation 21:1-5). Heaven is one big WOW! Way better than God's garden for Adam and Eve! Jesus will give God's children real and perfect bodies like his (Philippians 3:20-21). Sickness, quarrels, and death will never bother us again. We will love Jesus and each other fully (2 Corinthians 5:1-5).

Heaven, boring? Never! Just think—God designed our earthly bodies to taste honey, smell flowers, feel hugs, and see sunshine. How much more will our new bodies enjoy? Best of all, we will walk and talk with Jesus in God's beautiful new forever world (1 Corinthians 2:9). **Jesus's joy fills us now and forever.**

ENGAGE

Who doesn't look forward to Pixar movies, ice cream, and going to Disneyland? In heaven God's children will enjoy a better-than-ever thrill—Jesus! We will joyfully sit at Jesus's table and feast with him (Luke 22:29-30). Most of all we look forward to hearing Jesus speak words of life.

- In heaven we'll hear Jesus speak to us face to face. How can we get to know Jesus today?

- What one story does God's word tell us?

- Describe what you think it means that the joy we will have with Jesus in heaven will be better than any happiness we've ever known.

- What will be the best thing about heaven?

ENTER IN

Father God, heaven is more awesome than we can fully imagine. Living with you in heaven will be more exciting than anything in this life. Help us to think about the joys of heaven. And help us enjoy being with Jesus now, as we read your word. Amen.

JESUS PLANNED OUR JOY

FAMILY JOURNALING SPACE

IDEAS: Draw the disciples realising who Jesus is; or write what it will be like to see Jesus face to face; or something else…

DAY 29

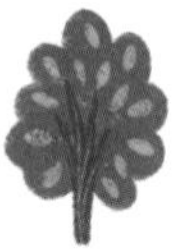

GOOD NEWS

EXPLORE

Read Luke 24:36 and 44-49

Compare what Jesus told his friends in verses 44-46 and what he told the two disciples in verses 25-31.

How would Jesus's promised gift help his friends? (verses 48-49)

EXPLAIN

The first Easter changed everything! Jesus told his friends to go and tell all people everywhere that God can forgive their sin. As people hear that Jesus died for them and rose again, God opens his children's hearts to believe. They turn from loving themselves most to loving Jesus, who loved them first. Jesus promised to help his friends tell others about him. He told them to wait for God's gift of the Holy Spirit.

The serpent mocks, *"What makes you think others will believe you?"* The truth is, our words alone can never make people believe in Jesus. Only the Holy Spirit can open hearts to believe (1 Corinthians 2:12). God's Spirit helps us live and speak the truth of the gospel (Romans 10:17).

Jesus always helps us to tell his good news (Acts 1:8). He makes us willing to go where he sends us. When we fear people, he strengthens us to trust him. God uses even our failures to show his grace (1 Timothy 1:15). He opens people's ears to hear when they don't like what we say. He turns the light switch on in their hearts to see and believe in Jesus (John 6:40). **Jesus helps us tell his good news.**

ENGAGE

God makes birds to fly and horses to run. He makes his children ready to share the good news of Jesus with others. Why can we pray and share God's good news boldly? Because Jesus has promised that everyone the Father draws to himself will come to believe (John 6:37-40).

- What does it mean to trust Jesus to help you talk with your friends about him?

- What gift did Jesus promise to give his friends?

- What would you tell a friend who thinks God's children should keep quiet about their faith?

- How does Jesus help us tell his good news?

ENTER IN

Father God, we often find it hard to talk to others about Jesus. Help us remember that everyone we meet may be someone who will become your child. Give us a desire to take a risk, knowing that you use our imperfect words and lives to open people's minds and hearts to faith in Jesus. Amen.

JESUS HELPS US TELL OTHERS

FAMILY JOURNALING SPACE

IDEAS: Draw people going all over the world with the good news; or write down some things you could tell your friends about Jesus; or something else...

DAY 30

EVERYTHING CHANGES

EXPLORE

Read Acts 1:3-11

Before Jesus went up into heaven, what did he tell his friends? (verses 4-5, 7-8)

After Jesus went up into heaven, what did the two men tell Jesus's friends? (verses 10-11)

EXPLAIN

Now, every day is better than Easter! 40 days after Jesus rose from death to new life, his friends watched him go up into heaven. Today Jesus is alive in heaven, praying for you and God's beautiful family (Hebrews 7:25). Today Jesus lives in all God's children through the Holy Spirit (John 14:15-21). The Holy Spirit frees our thoughts, words, and lives to change. We will be like Jesus (Colossians 3:1-4).

"You'll never change," the serpent scolds. The truth is, we have changed! God's Spirit lives in our hearts. God gives us new desires to love and please him. We may not always feel close to God. But the Holy Spirit helps us taste heaven in God's word. The serpent keeps lying. But we begin wanting a closer closeness to our Father. And the Holy Spirit helps us know there is more joy in pleasing God than in sin.

Today Jesus is King in our hearts. We can't wait for the day when Jesus will be King of his new earth. At last, life will be forever right. No more weeds. No sickness. No death. And no more serpent! God's better-than-ever Eden world will mean friendship with God forever! **Jesus is alive and changes everything!**

ENGAGE

The Holy Spirit makes the truth about Jesus more and more beautiful to us. Good grades, new clothes, devices, or winning prizes no longer make us the happiest. As we live to please Jesus we show him to our family and friends.

- The Holy Spirit helps us learn to make wise choices. Sometimes that means giving up what we love for what we will come to love better—pleasing God. If we give up something we love, what message does that send to those around us?

- What is Jesus doing today?

- When we receive Jesus as our Rescuer, the Holy Spirit puts his love into us. God's love gets us excited about helping our neighbor get what is best. How could you and your family show God's love to someone this week?

- Who is the Holy Spirit?

ENTER IN

Father God, we need Jesus to be King in our hearts. Help us listen to the Holy Spirit and live to please Jesus. Help us be Jesus's faithful witnesses with our lives and words. We look forward to the time when Jesus comes again as the King of a new earth. At last all will know he is the King of kings and Lord of lords! Amen.

JESUS CHANGES EVERYTHING

FAMILY JOURNALING SPACE

IDEAS: Draw your heart with a crown labeled "Jesus" above it; or write what you are willing to give up for Jesus if he asks you; or something else…

JESUS IS GOD´S AMAZING PLAN FOR EASTER!

HAPPY EASTER! This journaling space is for Easter Day.

FAMILY JOURNALING SPACE

IDEAS: Draw some important scenes from the Easter story; or list your favorite part of God's amazing plan for Easter; or something else…

EXTRA SPACE: This journaling space is for any day when you need more room.

FAMILY JOURNALING SPACE

EXTRA SPACE: This journaling space is for any day when you need more room.

FAMILY
JOURNALING
SPACE

FAMILY JOURNALING SPACE

EXTRA SPACE: This journaling space is for any day when you need more room.

ACKNOWLEDGMENTS

I am eternally grateful for my mentor and friend Sara Brigman, who faithfully reminds me to ask, "What is true about God?" and "What will change this to active voice?"

My heart overflows with gratitude for my godly son Benjamin Reaoch, who made use of his pastoral heart and theological mind to review this manuscript.

This book benefited in untold ways from Katy Morgan, whose big heart for God and keen eye for detail were very much appreciated. I have a deep appreciation for the amazing team at The Good Book Company. Each person used their God-given gifts and expertise to get this book into the hands of parents and kids.

1 Corinthians 1:4

thegoodbook
COMPANY

BIBLICAL | RELEVANT | ACCESSIBLE

At The Good Book Company, we are dedicated to helping Christians and local churches grow. We believe that God's growth process always starts with hearing clearly what he has said to us through his timeless word—the Bible.

Ever since we opened our doors in 1991, we have been striving to produce Bible-based resources that bring glory to God. We have grown to become an international provider of user-friendly resources to the Christian community, with believers of all backgrounds and denominations using our books, Bible studies, devotionals, evangelistic resources, and DVD-based courses.

We want to equip ordinary Christians to live for Christ day by day, and churches to grow in their knowledge of God, their love for one another, and the effectiveness of their outreach.

Call us for a discussion of your needs or visit one of our local websites for more information on the resources and services we provide.

Your friends at The Good Book Company

thegoodbook.com | thegoodbook.co.uk
thegoodbook.com.au | thegoodbook.co.nz
thegoodbook.co.in